CW01431734

The Truth Beyond Thought

Experiments To Rediscover Peace & Freedom

Vicki Montague

Copyright © 2025 by Vicki Montague

All rights reserved.

No part of this book may be reproduced in any form or by
any electronic or mechanical means, including information
storage and retrieval systems, without written permission
from the author, except for the use of brief quotations in a
book review.

Cover artwork by Vicki Montague

For all of my mentors, teachers and clients who have helped me to see more clearly what's true. It's because of you that this book has come into being.

And for Mark, Amelia & Arthur for having to listen to me talk about thought a lot when I first discovered the Three Principles! I love you all.

"What a liberation to realise that the 'voice in my head' is not who I am. Who am I then? The one who sees that."

— Eckhart Tolle

Contents

Foreword

A few months ago Vicki and I were talking and she was describing to me her love of simplicity.

Those who know her will not be surprised by this. She has a rare talent for seeing what is extraneous and ditching it in the most charming and effortless way. Her camper-van life, laser coaching and lived priorities are elegant testimony to this.

This talent and focus means that her life, her work, her relationships are a joyous celebration of the important and necessary.

Luckily for us, she doesn't just live this. She is also able to articulate it in words that convey the profound while always remaining colloquial and straight-forward.

This is what Vicki has done with this book. She has taken on THE most far reaching exploration for human kind - what we are and what is real.

This exploration, in less lovingly ruthless hands can become hopelessly convoluted and confusing.

Vicki, however, of course, has created a work of art of absolute simplicity and clarity. Through a focus on easy experiments, the practical and the every day, she opens up for all of us a whole new world.

The book takes just fifteen minutes to read.

Fifteen minutes in which a life can be turned upside down, inside out, shaken so that everything of illusory burden falls out of the pockets.

Leaving only what is required for joy, love, exploration and freedom.

We would not expect anything else from Vicki.

Clare Dimond

International coach, author, speaker and founder of the REAL platform aimed at helping individuals uncover their true nature.

Preface

This book came about as an experiment.

As someone who has been fond of science and experiments most of my life, I like to approach life as an experiment.

If you think experiments are for some boring school laboratory then let me introduce you to another possibility; they are a way of playing and having fun to discover something.

After many years of being told I should write a book, and many years of thinking I couldn't do that, one day I woke up with an idea; what if I just allowed some space for a book to be written?

And so, by allowing one hour a day for the duration of a week, most of this book came into form, seemingly of its own accord.

Of course, I, the human, translated ideas and thoughts into words on a page. But where those ideas and thoughts came from, I've no idea. They just came when they were given a space to come.

The way this book is set up is to act as a type of journal; or a book for you to write for yourself, with prompts.

I'm not going to tell you very much, but rather I'm going to direct you to look and explore for yourself and then write down what you discover.

I do understand that this might be frustrating at times, but rather than create new beliefs to live by, I want to encourage you to look and see what's true for yourself, and to record that in your own words. This will have way more impact on your life than anything I could ever tell you.

At the back of the book there are some resources that you might like to explore if you're left wanting more.

Introduction - "Not Enough"

Most of us are searching for something whether we know it or not.

We've grown up with a 'not enough' story ingrained within us which often means we spend our lives attempting to obtain more, in order to fix that apparent lack.

It might be more money, recognition, satisfaction, happiness, peace, love, contentment, fulfilment, acceptance or any number of other human desires.

What this means is that we spend most of our lives not being present, in an attempt to not feel and experience that apparent lack.

We dash around our lives over-eating, over-shopping, over-scrolling, over-drinking, taking drugs or whatever other habits we've innocently acquired to numb the pain of lack, or to not feel it.

But we didn't arrive in the world with this 'not enough' idea. It's something that we picked up after our arrival.

We're not going to go into the why.

We're not going to delve around in your past to work out why you don't feel enough.

None of that is needed.

Instead, I'm going to offer you some experiments to carry out.

My desire is that they will enable you to see what you really are; that you were never lacking and have always been 'enough'. And in the process, I hope you get at least a glimmer of the peace and freedom that you were born with and that always will be present no matter what is going on in your life.

When you come to nurture and pay attention to that, rather than to the stories of lack, your life will change. Don't take my word for it...let's get started!

Part One

Scattering Seeds For A New Life

Have you ever planted seeds, or known someone who has?

Without planting them, could any new plants have grown, or would you have just had the same old plants growing there?

Of course, you understand that you have to plant seeds for new plants to grow.

And it works the same with your life.

If you want things to be different, you need to plant some new seeds—what we'll call new ideas.

That's what this book is about. I'm going to gently offer some new ideas, and we'll see what grows.

Participation is required. It's no good just reading this book if you want to see things differently.

For that reason, I've created this book with spaces for you to keep track of your 'seeds'.

I highly recommend reading the book multiple times until what I'm pointing to becomes obvious and the 'seeds' grow into new 'plants'. It can take time sometimes for this process to happen.

I'll invite you to explore some new ideas. They might be really challenging, and you might want to walk away, or you might be aware of thoughts telling you it doesn't make sense and suggesting that you give up.

I know because I've been there! All I can say is to stay with it and don't be led by your thinking. If you feel like you need to walk away, do that and then come back another time.

And the best part of this process?

You don't have to work hard. You just need to

be open minded, curious and ready to see what's true.

I'm going to start by posing one simple and powerful question that we shall explore throughout the book...

What do you know about yourself without thoughts, ideas and beliefs?

Now we're ready to begin experimenting to see what's really true.

Part Two

What You Are Not

Imagine waking up one day and just knowing that you have everything you need to handle whatever comes your way.

That kind of knowing is possible for everyone. We just need to see through some ideas and beliefs that we've picked up during our time on this planet.

For most of our lives, we've believed things about ourselves—without ever really checking if they're true. So, let's start looking a bit closer at those beliefs.

Here are some of the common things we've believed:

1. That you are your thoughts.
2. That you are your body.
3. That you are the sum total of all the "I am..." statements like "I am shy," "I am bad at maths," or "I am too loud."
4. That you are separate - separate from nature, from others, and from the invisible, intelligent force that is life itself.

Let's explore some of these beliefs together to see if that's all we are. What you might discover is that you are way more than those things...

Experiment 1 - What Do I Believe About Myself?

Grab some post-it notes or small bits of paper, tape, and a pen.

On each piece, write one "I am..." statement that feels true about you. These are things that you've always thought about yourself and never questioned. Things like:

- "I am a girl."
- "I am shy."
- "I am bad at maths."
- "I am a student."
- "I am a teacher."

Write as many as you can think of, then stick them on your body. Yes, really!

Now look in the mirror.

How do you feel (besides a little silly)?

Do these labels feel good? Or do they feel heavy or limiting? Perhaps some feel good, and others feel like they limit you from doing what you'd love to do?

If they all feel light and wonderful—maybe you don't need this book! But if some feel uncomfortable or like they hold you back, you're in the right place.

Record what these labels feel like in the space below:

Experiment 2 - What's True?

Look at each one of those "I am..." statements you wrote. Ask yourself:

- Where did this come from?
- Did I create it, or did it just show up as thoughts that I believed?
- Did someone else tell me this and I believed it?
- Are they still true or are there times when they aren't true? Perhaps "I am shy" was one of yours but you notice now you're looking, that sometimes you're not shy.

Record what you find in the space below:

Here's what I found when I did this exercise:

- Most of my "I am" statements were heavy and unhelpful – they made me feel like lots of things weren't possible, that I was not good enough and that I was wrong in some way.
- They were thoughts. They were known to me through thought.
- Many came from what others said about me or from things that happened to me that I'd interpreted a certain way.
- I didn't choose to believe them—they just stuck and looked true.

A Pause

A Pause

Now take a break. Peel off the labels and save them somewhere or make a note of what you wrote down in the space at the back of this book.

Come back to this book in an hour, or a day or a week and try Experiments 1 & 2 again.

- Do the same labels come up?
- Do they change?

Notice that some might change and others might stay the same. If some change, ask yourself: *Can they really be who I am if they don't stay the same?*

Now, imagine all of those "I am..." statements being vacuumed away. Gone. Never to be experienced again.

Are you still here?

Yes?

Good.

Notice how all those labels have been like a cloak you've been wearing your whole life and now you're getting to see what lies beneath them.

Make a note of what you notice is still present without all those ideas about you...

Experiment 3 - A Closer Look At Thought

Now that we've played with ideas about what you believe about yourself, let's get curious about the building block of beliefs: **thought** itself.

Here are a few things to wonder about:

- Where do thoughts come from? And where do they go?
- Do you choose them or create them?
- Can you control them?
- If you did choose them or create them, why would some be unkind or unhelpful?

Thoughts are like weather passing through; they come and go on their own, don't they?

19

Try noticing:

- Did you choose your last thought?
- Can you predict your next one?

If you're noticing thoughts, can you really *be* them? Is there something more to you?

Record what you've discovered in the space below:

Experiment 4 - Examining The Body

Think about your body as a baby. Then as a child. And now.

Your body has changed so much.

Yet you still feel like *you,* don't you? Something about you hasn't ever changed, has it?

Something has stayed the same at all ages and appearances of your body.

Even if everything about your appearance were to shift—you'd still be "you" wouldn't you?

To explore this further I'd like you to consider what happens when a human or animal, or other living creature dies. Does their body disappear?

No.

The body stays but you know that 'they' are no longer there, don't you?

So if the body changes and it's 'left behind' when you die, can it really be who you are? Or are you something more than just the body?

Write down what you find when you explore this:

Part Three

What You Are

When all the "I am..." beliefs and labels and thoughts fall away, something remains.

You still know you exist.

You still know you're here.

This quiet knowing is not made of thought. It was there before your name, your age, your occupation or the "I am" ideas that you've picked up and believed about yourself.

I'm going to call it Aware. It's what everything else shows up in.

Some people call this god, consciousness, awareness, life, the intelligence of life, universe, unconditional love or peace.

Consider that in order for you to know anything, you need this. This comes before anything else; before a body, before thought, before you can know any objects or experiences.

Experiment 5 - What Are You Aware Of?

Pick up a book and ask yourself *Am I this book?*

No, of course not. You can see and hold it—it's something you're aware of.

Now look at your body.

Can you see it? Feel it?

Without all the thoughts you have about this body being 'yours', is the body also just something you're aware of—like the book?

What about thoughts?

Do you experience them? Do you feel them, hear them, know of them? Can they simply be something known within You; Aware?

You are Aware and then You (Aware) become aware of objects, including thoughts, a body and the outside world.

Write down the results of what you're discovering in the space below and we'll delve deeper...

Experiment 6 - What's Known Without Thought?

Close your eyes.

Are you still here?

Maybe there are thoughts that are saying things like "of course I'm here I can feel my body' or "of course I'm here because I can hear sounds around me."

But without paying attention to those thoughts would you still know you're here?

Is there something that effortlessly knows (is aware of) everything, without thought?

That effortlessly sees, hears, feels, smells, tastes and experiences everything, including thought?

That knowing might be who you really are...

Record what you're discovering in the space below:

Part Four

The Birth Of Self

When you entered the world, you were simply Aware with no ideas about who or what you were. You were pure, limitless potential.

Early in your life your family gave you a name. They referred to you as a girl or a boy and to other things too like eye colour and behaviour.

You weren't born knowing these things.

At some point you started to associate with them, you started to believe that was what you were because you'd been told it enough times.

Let's call that point the "birth of self." The moment you went from simply being Aware to identifying with certain things and not other things.

The moment the idea of separation was accepted 'You' innocently started to think of yourself as an individual, a body with thoughts, that was separate from others and separate from everything around you.

Or we could call it, the "birth of the ego; where the ego is simply a word to describe an identity made up of lots of "I am..." statements. All of which, I hope you are starting to see, were innocently given to you and innocently accepted, as true.

But when you look at them, could they all be changed or have many of them changed already?

Surely anything that changes can't be all you are?

So... what has never changed?

A knowing that you are; that you exist?

You know you're here. You're Aware.

You have always been Aware. That has never changed.

Part Five

Aware As A Screen

If who you are is simply Aware what does that mean about you and all your problems?

Are they 'yours' or are they simply what's appearing in the space of Aware, now?

Another way I like to consider Aware is like a blank screen; like a cinema screen.

Imagine a cinema screen now.

Movies are experienced on the screen—they can be sad, joyful or dramatic—much like the experiences of your life - but the screen stays the same and is not impacted by the movie playing on it.

You are like the screen.

Thoughts, feelings and things are experienced; witnessed, but they're not you.

You are that which knows of those things; which is aware of those things.

The quiet space in which all things appear.

Part Six

Aware As The Ocean

Another way to consider Aware is to liken it to the ocean.

Each wave you see seems to be unique and separate from the ocean.

But each wave is actually made from ocean. A wave can never be separate from the ocean. It's an appearance of ocean that is there one moment and then dissolves back into ocean in the next moment; a temporary form, made from ocean that dissolves back into ocean.

Each human form, and indeed all forms (even 'thought forms'), appear to be separate things.

However, they are all made from Aware. They cannot exist without Aware, can they? Take Aware away and there is no knowing of these forms is there?

So, you appear to be a separate, unique entity but in actual fact, like a wave in the ocean, you are never separate from what you are made of.

Part Seven

All of It

So... I hope what you've discovered in this short collection of experiments is that you are not just your thoughts and not just your body, although you experience both as who you are.

What I'm pointing to is that these things are not *all* you are. They are *known* in what you are.

You are Aware and you believe yourself to be a human, separate from Aware (or consciousness or unconditional love or peace or the intelligence of life or god...whatever word speaks to you).

In a practical sense, knowing more often that you are Aware, into which everything appears, including 'your' body, thoughts and sensations means that those things can be experienced with less struggle and more ease, more of the time.

You can have all experiences because you start to see that they are simply things appearing within You, Aware. And at any time, when thoughts or feelings feel overwhelming, you can remember that you are simply aware of those things and come back to peace.

You can feel, laugh, cry, create, rest and resist. You can experience it all.

Like an actor in a play—fully immersed in the experience yet never forgetting who they really are.

When not caught up in thoughts and beliefs, everything is available to you. The solution to every problem lies in Aware because Aware contains everything.

Try it out for yourself.

Disengage with all thoughts (ideas, concepts and beliefs – which are simply thoughts) just for a moment and become present to what is, right here, right now.

Is there a problem without thought?

How does that feel?

What do you know?

Is peace and freedom present?

Make a note below of what this is for you, in your words:

Conclusion

Next time a thought or sensation feels heavy, and discomfort is present, pause.

Ask: *What's true right now, without thought?*

You are not the thought.

You are aware of it.

You are not the feeling.

You are aware of it.

You are not a fixed identity. You are not a collection of beliefs. You are effortlessly Aware of all of it.

And from here, you can fully live.

Not because you've figured it all out—because you've remembered who you've always been.

And life immediately becomes less serious and more fun.

I look forward to this for you.

Further Reading & Resources

I have a selection of free resources including blogs, online video courses and podcasts on my website:

https://freefromlimits.co.uk.

I also have an extensive range of videos on my YouTube channel:

https://www.youtube.com/@VickiMontague-FreeFromLimits.

If you'd like to read more, any books from the following authors will provide you with more information about what you might have discovered from reading this book.

Allow yourself to be drawn to a particular author and book. You'll know which is right for you:

Clare Dimond

Eckhart Tolle

Salvadore Poe

Rupert Spira

John Wheeler

Sydney Banks

Michael Neill

Amy Johnson

George and/or Linda and/or Jack Pransky

Dicken Bettinger

Steve Chandler

Michael Singer

About the Author

As a Wellbeing & Possibility Coach, Vicki expertly guides people using gentle curiosity, deep listening and disruptive questions, back to their unlimited true potential; to what has always been available but unseen.

By utilising a radical new paradigm of psychological understanding, a fresh perspective on problems becomes available and things that appeared impossible become possible.

She works with curious, open-minded adults who know there is more to life than their current experience and who are ready to start thriving.

They may be creatives who are experiencing creative blocks, business owners or employees paralysed by fear and insecurity or people whose lives have become restricted through physical and/or mental ill-health.

Your Notes & Reflections

Printed in Dunstable, United Kingdom

64122423R00047